MOTLEY
AND OTHER POEMS

MOTLEY

AND OTHER POEMS

BY

WALTER DE LA MARE

NEW YORK

HENRY HOLT AND COMPANY

1918

NOTE

THE author wishes to thank the Editors
of the *English Review*, the *Times*, the *New
Statesman*, *Form*, the *Gipsy*, the *Yale Review*, and the *Westminster Gazette* for
permission to reprint poems included in
this volume.

A selection from among the poems included in this volume has been published
in a limited edition in a volume issued by
the Beaumont Press.

CONTENTS

viii   *Contents*

Contents

THE LITTLE SALAMANDER

TO MARGOT

WHEN I go free,
I think 'twill be
A night of stars and snow,
And the wild fires of frost shall light
My footsteps as I go;
Nobody—nobody will be there
With groping touch, or sight,
To see me in my bush of hair
Dance burning through the night.

THE LINNET

Upon this leafy bush
With thorns and roses in it,
Flutters a thing of light,
A twittering linnet.
And all the throbbing world
Of dew and sun and air
By this small parcel of life
Is made more fair;
As if each bramble-spray
And mounded gold-wreathed furze,
Harebell and little thyme,
Were only hers;
As if this beauty and grace
Did to one bird belong,
And, at a flutter of wing,
Might vanish in song.

THE SUNKEN GARDEN

SPEAK not—whisper not;
Here bloweth thyme and bergamot;
Softly on the evening hour,
Secret herbs their spices shower,
Dark-spiked rosemary and myrrh,
Lean-stalked, purple lavender;
Hides within her bosom, too,
All her sorrows, bitter rue.

Breathe not—trespass not;
Of this green and darkling spot,
Latticed from the moon's beams,
Perchance a distant dreamer dreams;
Perchance upon its darkening air,
The unseen ghosts of children fare,
Faintly swinging, sway and sweep,
Like lovely sea-flowers in its deep;
While, unmoved, to watch and ward,
'Mid its gloomed and daisied sward,
Stands with bowed and dewy head
That one little leaden Lad.

THE RIDDLERS

' Thou solitary!' the Blackbird cried,
' I, from the happy Wren,
Linnet and Blackcap, Woodlark, Thrush,
Perched all upon a sweetbrier bush,
Have come at cold of midnight-tide
To ask thee, Why and when
Grief smote thy heart so thou dost sing
In solemn hush of evening,
So sorrowfully, lovelorn Thing—
Nay, nay, not sing, but rave, but wail,
Most melancholic Nightingale?
Do not the dews of darkness steep
All pinings of the day in sleep?
Why, then, when rocked in starry nest
We mutely couch, secure, at rest,
Doth thy lone heart delight to make
Music for sorrow's sake?'

A Moon was there.   So still her beam,
It seemed the whole world lay a-dream,
Lulled by the watery sea.
And from her leafy night-hung nook
Upon this stranger soft did look
The Nightingale: sighed he:—

' 'Tis strange, my friend; the Kingfisher
But yestermorn conjured me here
Out of his green and gold to say
Why thou, in splendour of the noon,
Wearest of colour but golden shoon,
And else dost thee array
In a most sombre suit of black?
" Surely," he sighed, " some load of grief,
Past all our thinking—and belief—
Must weigh upon his back! "
Do, then, in turn, tell me, If joy
Thy heart as well as voice employ,
Why dost thou now, most Sable, shine
In plumage woefuller far than mine?
Thy silence is a sadder thing
Than any dirge I sing! '

Thus then these two small birds, perched there,
Breathed a strange riddle both did share
Yet neither could expound.
And we—who sing but as we can,
In the small knowledge of a man—
Have we an answer found?
Nay, some are happy whose delight
Is hid even from themselves from sight;
And some win peace who spend
The skill of words to sweeten despair
Of finding consolation where
Life has but one dark end;
Who, in rapt solitude, tell o'er
A tale, as lovely as forlore,
Into the midnight air.

MOONLIGHT

THE far moon maketh lovers wise
   In her pale beauty trembling down,
Lending curved cheeks, dark lips, dark eyes,
   A strangeness not their own.
And, though they shut their lids to kiss,
In starless darkness peace to win,
Even on that secret world from this
   Her twilight enters in.

THE BLIND BOY

'I HAVE no master,' said the Blind Boy,
My mother, "Dame Venus," they do call;
Cowled in this hood, she sent me begging
For whate'er in pity may befall.

'Hard was her visage, me adjuring,—
"Have no fond mercy on the kind!
Here be sharp arrows, bunched in quiver,
Draw close ere striking—thou art blind."

'So stand I here, my woes entreating,
In this dark alley, lest the Moon
Point with her sparkling my barbed armoury,
Shine on my silver-lacèd shoon.

'Oh, sir, unkind this Dame to me-ward;
Of the salt billow was her birth. . . .
In your sweet charity draw nearer
The saddest rogue on Earth!'

THE QUARRY

You hunted me with all the pack,
Too blind, too blind, to see
By no wild hope of force or greed
Could you make sure of me.

And like a phantom through the glades,
With tender breast aglow,
The goddess in me laughed to hear
Your horns a-roving go.

She laughed to think no mortal e'er
By dint of mortal flesh
The very Cause that was the Hunt
One moment could enmesh:

That though with captive limbs I lay,
Stilled breath and vanquished eyes,
He that hunts Love with horse and hound
Hunts out his heart and eyes.

MRS. GRUNDY

'STEP very softly, sweet Quiet-foot,
Stumble not, whisper not, smile not:
By this dark ivy stoop cheek and brow.
Still even thy heart! What seest thou?'

'High-coifed, broad-browed, aged, suave yet
    grim,
A large flat face, eyes keenly dim,
Staring at nothing—that's me!—and yet,
With a hate one could never, no, never for-
    get . . .'

'This is my world, my garden, my home,
Hither my father bade mother to come
And bear me out of the dark into light,
And happy I was in her tender sight.

'And then, thou frail flower, she died and
    went,
Forgetting my pitiless banishment,

And that Old Woman—an Aunt—she said,
Came hither, lodged, fattened, and made her
    bed.

'Oh yes, thou most blessed, from Monday to
    Sunday
Has lived on me, preyed on me, Mrs. Grundy:
Called me, "dear Nephew"; on each of those
    chairs
Has gloated in righteousness, heard my
    prayers.

Why didst thou dare the thorns of the grove,
Timidest trespasser, huntress of love?
Now thou hast peeped, and now dost know
What kind of creature is thine for foe.

'Not that she'll tear out thy innocent eyes,
Poison thy mouth with deviltries.
Watch thou, wait thou: soon will begin
The guile of a voice: hark! . . .' 'Come in,
    Come in!'

THE TRYST

FLEE into some forgotten night and be
Of all dark long my moon-bright company:
Beyond the rumour even of Paradise come,
There, out of all remembrance, make our
      home:
Seek we some close hid shadow for our lair,
Hollowed by Noah's mouse beneath the chair
Wherein the Omnipotent, in slumber bound,
Nods till the piteous Trump of Judgment
      sound.
Perchance Leviathan of the deep sea
Would lease a lost mermaiden's grot to me,
There of your beauty we would joyance
      make—
A music wistful for the sea-nymph's sake:
Haply Elijah, o'er his spokes of fire,
Cresting steep Leo, or the heavenly Lyre,
Spied, tranced in azure of inanest space,
Some eyrie hostel, meet for human grace,

Where two might happy be—just you and I—
Lost in the uttermost of Eternity.

Think! in Time's smallest clock's minutest beat
Might there not rest be found for wandering
    feet?
Or, 'twixt the sleep and wake of a Helen's
    dream,
Silence wherein to sing love's requiem?

No, no. Nor earth, nor air, nor fire, nor deep
Could lull poor mortal longingness asleep.
Somewhere there Nothing is; and there lost
    Man
Shall win what changeless vague of peace he
    can.

ALONE

THE abode of the nightingale is bare,
Flowered frost congeals in the gelid air,
The fox howls from his frozen lair:
> Alas, my loved one is gone,
> I am alone:
> It is winter.

Once the pink cast a winy smell,
The wild bee hung in the hyacinth bell,
Light in effulgence of beauty fell:
> Alas, my loved one is gone,
> I am alone:
> It is winter.

My candle a silent fire doth shed,
Starry Orion hunts o'erhead;
Come moth, come shadow, the world is dead:
> Alas, my loved one is gone,
> I am alone:
> It is winter.

THE EMPTY HOUSE

See this house, how dark it is
Beneath its vast-boughed trees!
Not one trembling leaflet cries
To that Watcher in the skies—
' Remove, remove thy searching gaze,
Innocent, of heaven's ways,
Brood not, Moon, so wildly bright,
On secrets hidden from sight.'

' Secrets,' sighs the night-wind,
' Vacancy is all I find;
Every keyhole I have made
Wail a summons, faint and sad,
No voice ever answers me,
      Only vacancy.'
' Once, once . . .' the cricket shrills,
And far and near the quiet fills
With its tiny voice, and then
      Hush falls again.

15

Mute shadows creeping slow
Mark how the hours go.
Every stone is mouldering slow.
And the least winds that blow
Some minutest atom shake,
Some fretting ruin make
In roof and walls. How black it is
Beneath these thick-boughed trees!

MISTRESS FELL

'Whom seek you here, sweet Mistress Fell?'
'One who loved me passing well.
Dark his eye, wild his face—
Stranger, if in this lonely place
Bide such an one, then, prythee, say
I am come here to-day.'

'Many his like, Mistress Fell?'
'I did not look, so cannot tell.
Only this I surely know,
When his voice called me, I must go;
Touched me his fingers, and my heart
Leapt at the sweet pain's smart.'

'Why did he leave you, Mistress Fell?'
'Magic laid its dreary spell.—
Stranger, he was fast asleep;
Into his dream I tried to creep;
Called his name, soft was my cry:
He answered—not one sigh.

' The flower and the thorn are here;
Falleth the night-dew, cold and clear;
Out of her bower the bird replies,
Mocking the dark with ecstasies,
See how the earth's green grass doth grow,
Praising what sleeps below!

' Thus have they told me. And I come,
As flies the wounded wild-bird home.
Not tears I give; but all that he
Clasped in his arms, sweet charity;
All that he loved—to him I bring
For a close whispering.'

THE GHOST

'Who knocks?' 'I, who was beautiful,
Beyond all dreams to restore,
I, from the roots of the dark thorn am hither,
And knock on the door.'

'Who speaks?' 'I—once was my speech
Sweet as the bird's on the air.
When echo lurks by the waters to heed;
'Tis I speak thee fair.'

'Dark is the hour!' 'Ay, and cold.'
'Lone is my house.' 'Ah, but mine?'
'Sight, touch, lips, eyes yearned in vain.'
'Long dead these to thine . . .'

Silence. Still faint on the porch
Brake the flames of the stars.
In gloom groped a hope-wearied hand
Over keys, bolts, and bars.

A face peered.   All the grey night
In chaos of vacancy shone;
Nought but vast Sorrow was there—
The sweet cheat gone.

THE STRANGER

In the woods as I did walk,
Dappled with the moon's beam,
I did with a Stranger talk,
And his name was Dream.

Spurred his heel, dark his cloak,
Shady-wide his bonnet's brim;
His horse beneath a silvery oak
Grazed as I talked with him.

Softly his breast-brooch burned and shone;
Hill and deep were in his eyes;
One of his hands held mine, and one
The fruit that makes men wise.

Wonderly strange was earth to see,
Flowers white as milk did gleam;
Spread to Heaven the Assyrian Tree,
Over my head with Dream.

Dews were still betwixt us twain;
Stars a trembling beauty shed;
Yet—not a whisper comes again
Of the words he said.

BETRAYAL

SHE will not die, they say,
She will but put her beauty by
    And hie away.

Oh, but her beauty gone, how lonely
Then will seem all reverie,
    How black to me!

All things will sad be made
And every hope a memory,
    All gladness dead.'

Ghosts of the past will know
My weakest hour, and whisper to me,
    And coldly go.

And hers in deep of sleep,
Clothed in its mortal beauty I shall see,
    And, waking, weep.

Naught will my mind then find
In man's false Heaven my peace to be:
    All blind, and blind.

THE CAGE

WHY did you flutter in vain hope, poor bird,
Hard-pressed in your small cage of clay?
'Twas but a sweet, false echo that you heard,
    Caught only a feint of day.

Still is the night all dark, a homeless dark.
Burn yet the unanswering stars. And silence
    brings
The same sea's desolate surge—*sans* bound or
    mark—
        Of all your wanderings.

Fret now no more; be still. Those steadfast
    eyes,
Those folded hands, they cannot set you free;
Only with beauty wake wild memories—
Sorrow for where you are, for where you
    would be.

THE REVENANT

O ALL ye fair ladies with your colours and
    your graces,
And your eyes clear in flame of candle and
    hearth,
To'rd the dark of this old window lift not up
    your smiling faces,
Where a Shade stands forlorn from the cold
    of the earth.

God knows I could not rest for one I still was
    thinking of;
Like a rose sheathed in beauty her spirit was
    to me;
Now out of unforgottenness a bitter draught
    I'm drinking of,
'Tis sad of such beauty unremembered to be.

Men all are shades, O Women.—Winds wist
    not of the way they blow.
Apart from your kindness, life's at best but a
    snare.

Though a tongue now past praise this bitter
    thing doth say, I know
What solitude means, and how, homeless, I
    fare.

Strange, strange, are ye all—except in beauty
    shared with her—
Since I seek one I loved, yet was faithless to
    in death.
Not life enough I heaped, so thus my heart
    must fare with her,
Now wrapt in the gross clay, bereft of life's
    breath.

MUSIC

When music sounds, gone is the earth I know,
And all her lovely things even lovelier grow;
Her flowers in vision flame, her forest trees,
Lift burdened branches, stilled with ecstasies.

When music sounds, out of the water rise
Naiads whose beauty dims my waking eyes,
Rapt in strange dream burns each enchanted
        face,
With solemn echoing stirs their dwelling-place.

When music sounds, all that I was I am
Ere to this haunt of brooding dust I came;
While from Time's woods break into distant
        song
The swift-winged hours, as I hasten along.

THE REMONSTRANCE

I WAS at peace until you came
And set a careless mind aflame.
I lived in quiet; cold, content;
All longing in safe banishment,
Until your ghostly lips and eyes
   Made wisdom unwise.

Naught was in me to tempt your feet
To seek a lodging. Quite forgot
Lay the sweet solitude we two
In childhood used to wander through;
Time's cold had closed my heart about;
   And shut you out.

Well, and what then? . . . O vision grave,
Take all the little all I have!
Strip me of what in voiceless thought
Life's kept of life, unhoped, unsought!—
Reverie and dream that memory must
   Hide deep in dust!

This only I say,—Though cold and bare
The haunted house you have chosen to share,
Still 'neath its walls the moonbeam goes
And trembles on the untended rose;
Still o'er its broken roof-tree rise
The starry arches of the skies;
And 'neath your lightest word shall be
The thunder of an ebbing sea.

NOCTURNE

'Tis not my voice now speaks; but as a bird
In darkling forest hollows a sweet throat—
Pleads on till distant echo too hath heard
      And doubles every note:
So love that shrouded dwells in mystery
      Would cry and waken thee.

Thou Solitary, stir in thy still sleep;
All the night waits thee, yet thou still dream'st
      on.
Furtive the shadows that about thee creep,
And cheat the shining footsteps of the moon:
Unseal thine eyes, it is my heart that sings,
      And beats in vain its wings.

Lost in heaven's vague, the stars burn softly
      thro'
The world's dark latticings, we prisoned stray
Within its lovely labyrinth, and know
      Mute seraphs guard the way
Even from silence unto speech, from love
To that self's self it still is dreaming of.

THE EXILE

I AM that Adam who, with Snake for guest,
Hid anguished eyes upon Eve's piteous breast.
I am that Adam who, with broken wings,
Fled from the Seraph's brazen trumpetings.
Betrayed and fugitive, I still must roam
A world where sin—and beauty—whisper of
    Home.

Oh, from wide circuit, shall at length I see
Pure daybreak lighten again on Eden's tree?
Loosed from remorse and hope and love's
    distress,
Enrobe me again in my lost nakedness?
No more with wordless grief a loved one
    grieve,
But to heaven's nothingness re-welcome Eve?

THE UNCHANGING

AFTER the songless rose of evening,
    Night quiet, dark, still,
In nodding cavalcade advancing
    Starred the deep hill:
You, in the valley standing,
    In your quiet wonder took
All that glamour, peace, and mystery
    In one grave look.
Beauty hid your naked body,
    Time dreamed in your bright hair,
In your eyes the constellations
    Burned far and fair.

NIGHTFALL

The last light fails—that shallow pool of day!
The coursers of the dark stamp down to drink,
Arch their wild necks, lift their wild heads and
　　neigh;
Their drivers, gathering at the water-brink,
With eyes ashine from out their clustering hair,
Utter their hollow speech, or gaze afar,
Rapt in irradiant reverie, to where
Languishes, lost in light, the evening star.

Come the wood-nymphs to dance within the
　　glooms,
Calling these charioteers with timbrels' din;
Ashen with twilight the dark forest looms
O'er the nocturnal beasts that prowl within
Thorn-roofèd thicket, where sweet waters
　　gush.
Resounding roar wild torrent, hungry throat;
While in the dew-drowsed branches' ebon hush,
Pouring lament of joy, the night birds float.

' O glory of beauty which the world makes
    fair ! '
Pant they their serenading on the air.

Sound the loud hooves, and all abroad the sky
The lusty charioteers their stations take;
Planet to planet do the sweet Loves fly,
And in the zenith silver music wake.
Cities of men, in blindness hidden low,
Fume their faint flames to that arched
    firmament,
But all the dwellers in the lonely know
The unearthly are abroad, and weary and
    spent,
With rush extinguished, to their dreaming go.
And world and night and star-enclustered
    space
The glory of beauty are in one enravished face.

INVOCATION

THE burning fire shakes in the night,
 On high her silver candles gleam,
With far-flung arms enflamed with light,
 The trees are lost in dream.

Come in thy beauty! 'tis my love,
 Lost in far-wandering desire,
Hath in the darkling deep above
 Set stars and kindled fire.

EYES

O STRANGE devices that alone divide
The seër from the seen—
The very highway of earth's pomp and pride
That lies between
The traveller and the cheating, sweet delight
Of where he longs to be,
But which, bound hand and foot, he, close on
    night,
Can only see.

LIFE

HEARKEN, O dear, now strikes the hour we
    die;
We, who in one strange kiss
Have proved a dream the world's realities,
Turned each from other's darkness with a sigh,
Need heed no more of life, waste no more
    breath
On any other journey, but of death.

And yet: Oh, know we well
How each of us must prove Love's infidel;
Still out of ecstasy turn trembling back
To earth's same empty track
Of leaden day by day, and hour by hour,
    and be
Of all things lovely the cold mortuary.

THE DISGUISE

WHY in my heart, O Grief,
Dost thou in beauty bide?
Dead is my well-content,
And buried deep my pride.
Cold are their stones, beloved,
To hand and side.

The shadows of even are gone,
Shut are the day's clear flowers,
Now have her birds left mute
Their singing bowers,
Lone shall we be, we twain,
In the night hours.

Thou with thy cheek on mine,
And dark hair loosed, shalt see
Take the far stars for fruit
The cypress tree,
And in the yew's black
Shall the moon be.

38

We will tell no old tales,
Nor heed if in wandering air
Die a lost song of love
Or the once fair;
Still as well-water be
The thoughts we share!

And, while the ghosts keep
Tryst from chill sepulchres,
Dreamless our gaze shall sleep,
And sealed our ears;
Heart unto heart will speak,
Without tears.

O, thy veiled, lovely face—
Joy's strange disguise—
Shall be the last to fade
From these rapt eyes,
Ere the first dart of daybreak
Pierce the skies.

VAIN QUESTIONING

WHAT needest thou?—a few brief hours of
    rest
Wherein to seek thyself in thine own breast;
A transient silence wherein truth could say
Such was thy constant hope, and this thy
    way?—
        O burden of life that is
        A livelong tangle of perplexities!

What seekest thou?—a truce from that thou
    art;
Some steadfast refuge from a fickle heart;
Still to be thou, and yet no thing of scorn,
To find no stay here, and yet not forlorn?—
        O riddle of life that is
        An endless war 'twixt contrarieties.

Leave this vain questioning. Is not sweet the
    rose?
Sings not the wild bird ere to rest he goes?
Hath not in miracle brave June returned?
Burns not her beauty as of old it burned?
    O foolish one to roam
      So far in thine own mind away from
      home!

Where blooms the flower when her petals fade,
Where sleepeth echo by earth's music made,
Where all things transient to the changeless
    win,
There waits the peace thy spirit dwelleth in.

VIGIL

Dark is the night,
The fire burns faint and low,
Hours—days—years,
Into grey ashes go;
I strive to read,
But sombre is the glow.

Thumbed are the pages,
And the print is small;
Mocking the winds
That from the darkness call;
Feeble the fire that lends
Its light withal.

O ghost, draw nearer;
Let thy shadowy hair,
Blot out the pages
That we cannot share;
Be ours the one last leaf
By Fate left bare!

Let's Finis scrawl,
And then Life's book put by;
Turn each to each
In all simplicity:
Ere the last flame is gone
To warm us by.

THE OLD MEN

OLD and alone, sit we,
Caged, riddle-rid men;
Lost to earth's 'Listen!' and 'See!'
Thought's 'Wherefore?' and 'When?'

Only far memories stray
Of a past once lovely, but now
Wasted and faded away,
Like green leaves from the bough.

Vast broods the silence of night,
The ruinous moon
Lifts on our faces her light,
Whence all dreaming is gone.

We speak not; trembles each head;
In their sockets our eyes are still;
Desire as cold as the dead;
Without wonder or will.

And One, with a lanthorn, draws near,
At clash with the moon in our eyes:
'Where art thou?' he asks: 'I am here,'
One by one we arise.

And none lifts a hand to withhold
A friend from the touch of that foe:
Heart cries unto heart, 'Thou art old!'
Yet reluctant, we go.

THE DREAMER

O THOU who giving helm and sword,
Gav'st, too, the rusting rain,
And starry dark's all tender dews
    To blunt and stain:

Out of the battle I am sped,
Unharmed, yet stricken sore;
A living shape 'mid whispering shades
    On Lethe's shore.

No trophy in my hands I bring,
To this sad, sighing stream,
The neighings and the trumps and cries
    Were but a dream—a dream.

Traitor to life, of life betrayed—
O, of thy mercy deep,
A dream my all, the all I ask
    Is sleep.

HAPPY ENGLAND

Now each man's mind all Europe is:
    Boding and fear in dread array
Daze every heart: O grave and wise,
    Abide in hope the judgment day.

This war of millions in arms
    In myriad replica we wage;
Unmoved, then, Soul, by earth's alarms
    The dangers of the dark engage.

Remember happy England: keep
    For her bright cause thy latest breath;
Her peace that long hath lulled to sleep,
    May now exact the sleep of death.

Her woods and wilds, her loveliness,
    With harvest now are richly at rest;
Safe in her isled securities,
    Thy children's heaven is her breast.

O what a deep contented night
    The sun from out her Eastern seas
Would bring the dust which in her sight
    Had given its all for these!

MOTLEY

Come, Death, I'd have a word with thee;
And thou, poor Innocency;
And Love—a lad with broken wing;
And Pity, too:
The Fool shall sing to you,
As Fools will sing.

Ay, music hath small sense,
And a tune's soon told,
And Earth is old,
And my poor wits are dense;
Yet have I secrets,—dark, my dear,
To breathe you all: Come near.
And lest some hideous listener tells,
I'll ring my bells.

They're all at war!—
Yes, yes, their bodies go
'Neath burning sun and icy star
To chaunted songs of woe,

Dragging cold cannon through a mire
Of rain and blood and spouting fire,
The new moon glinting hard on eyes
Wide with insanities!

Hush! . . . I use words
I hardly know the meaning of;
And the mute birds
Are glancing at Love
From out their shade of leaf and flower,
Trembling at treacheries
Which even in noonday cower.
Heed, heed not what I said
Of frenzied hosts of men,
More fools than I,
On envy, hatred fed,
Who kill, and die—
Spake I not plainly, then?
Yet Pity whispered, 'Why?'

Thou silly thing, off to thy daisies go.
Mine was not news for child to know,
And Death—no ears hath. He hath supped
        where creep
Eyeless worms in hush of sleep;

Yet, when he smiles, the hand he draws
Athwart his grinning jaws—
Faintly the thin bones rattle, and—There,
    there;
Hearken how my bells in the air
Drive away care! . . .

Nay, but a dream I had
Of a world all mad.
Not simple happy mad like me,
Who am mad like an empty scene
Of water and willow tree,
Where the wind hath been;
But that foul Satan-mad,
Who rots in his own head,
And counts the dead,
Not honest one—and two—
But for the ghosts they were,
Brave, faithful, true,
When, head in air,
In Earth's clear green and blue
Heaven they did share
With beauty who bade them there. . . .

There, now! Death goes—
Mayhap I've wearied him.
Ay, and the light doth dim,
And asleep's the rose,
And tired Innocence
In dreams is hence. . . .
Come, Love, my lad,
Nodding that drowsy head,
'Tis time thy prayers were said!

THE MARIONETTES

Let the foul Scene proceed:
  There's laughter in the wings;
'Tis sawdust that they bleed,
  But a box Death brings.

How rare a skill is theirs
  These extreme pangs to show,
How real a frenzy wears
  Each feigner of woe!

Gigantic dins uprise!
  Even the gods must feel
A smarting of the eyes
  As these fumes upsweal.

Strange, such a Piece is free,
  While we Spectators sit,
Aghast at its agony,
  Yet absorbed in it!

53

Dark is the outer air,
  Coldly the night draughts blow,
Mutely we stare, and stare
  At the frenzied Show.

Yet heaven hath its quiet shroud
  Of deep, immutable blue—
We cry ' An end! ' We are bowed
  By the dread, ' 'Tis true! '

While the Shape who hoofs applause
  Behind our deafened ear,
Hoots—angel-wise—' the Cause! '
  And affright ev'n fear.

TO E. T.: 1917

You sleep too well—too far away,
For sorrowing word to soothe or wound;
Your very quiet seems to say
How longed-for a peace you have found.

Else, had not death so lured you on,
You would have grieved—'twixt joy and
    fear—
To know how my small loving son
Had wept for you, my dear.

APRIL MOON

Roses are sweet to smell and see,
　　And lilies on the stem;
But rarer, stranger buds there be,
　　And she was like to them.

The little moon that April brings,
　　More lovely shade than light,
That, setting, silvers lonely hills
　　Upon the verge of night—

Close to the world of my poor heart
　　So stole she, still and clear;
Now that she's gone, O dark, and dark,
　　The solitude—the fear.

THE FOOL'S SONG

Never, no never, listen too long,
To the chattering wind in the willows, the
    night bird's song.

'Tis sad in sooth to lie under the grass,
But none too gladsome to wake and grow cold
    where life's shadows pass.

Dumb the old Toll-Woman squats,
And, for every green copper battered and worn,
    doles out Nevers and Nots.

I know a Blind Man, too,
Who with a sharp ear listens and listens the
    whole world through.

Oh, sit we snug to our feast,
With platter and finger and spoon—and good
    victuals at least.

CLEAR EYES

CLEAR eyes do dim at last,
And cheeks outlive their rose.
Time, heedless of the past,
No loving-kindness knows;
Chill unto mortal lip
Still Lethe flows.

Griefs, too, but brief while stay,
And sorrow, being o'er,
Its salt tears shed away,
Woundeth the heart no more.
Stealthily lave those waters
That solemn shore.

Ah, then, sweet face burn on,
While yet quick memory lives!
And Sorrow, ere thou art gone,
Know that my heart forgives—
Ere yet, grown cold in peace,
It loves not, nor grieves.

58

DUST TO DUST

HEAVENLY Archer, bend thy bow;
Now the flame of life burns low,
Youth is gone; I, too, would go.

Ever Fortune leads to this:
Harsh or kind, at last she is
Murderess of all ecstasies.

Yet the spirit, dark, alone,
Bound in sense, still hearkens on
For tidings of a bliss foregone.

Sleep is well for dreamless head,
At no breath astonished,
From the Gardens of the Dead.

I the immortal harps hear ring,
By Babylon's river languishing.
Heavenly Archer, loose thy string.

THE THREE STRANGERS

FAR are those tranquil hills,
Dyed with fair evening's rose;
On urgent, secret errand bent,
    A traveller goes.

Approach him strangers three,
Barefooted, cowled; their eyes
Scan the lone, hastening solitary
    With dumb surmise.

One instant in close speech
With them he doth confer:
God-sped, he hasteneth on,
    That anxious traveller . . .

I was that man—in a dream:
And each world's night in vain
I patient wait on sleep to unveil
Those vivid hills again.

Would that they three could know
How yet burns on in me
Love—from one lost in Paradise—
For their grave courtesy.

ALEXANDER

It was the Great Alexander,
Capped with a golden helm,
Sate in the ages, in his floating ship,
   In a dead calm.

Voices of sea-maids singing
Wandered across the deep:
The sailors labouring on their oars
   Rowed, as in sleep.

All the high pomp of Asia,
Charmed by that siren lay,
Out of their weary and dreaming minds,
   Faded away.

Like a bold boy sate their Captain,
His glamour withered and gone,
In the souls of his brooding mariners,
   While the song pined on.

Time, like a falling dew,
Life, like the scene of a dream,
Laid between slumber and slumber,
   Only did seem. . . .

O Alexander, then,
In all us mortals too,
Wax thou not bold—too bold
   On the wave dark-blue!

Come the calm, infinite night,
Who then will hear
Aught save the singing
   Of the sea-maids clear?

THE REAWAKENING

GREEN in light are the hills, and a calm wind
    flowing
Filleth the void with a flood of the fragrance
    of Spring;
Wings in this mansion of life are coming and
    going,
Voices of unseen loveliness carol and sing.

Coloured with buds of delight the boughs are
    swaying,
Beauty walks in the woods, and wherever she
    rove
Flowers from wintry sleep, her enchantment
    obeying,
Stir in the deep of her dream, reawaken to
    love.

Oh, now begone sullen care—this light is my
    seeing;
I am the palace, and mine are its windows and
    walls;

Daybreak is come, and life from the darkness
    of being
Springs, like a child from the womb, when the
    lonely one calls.

THE VACANT DAY

As I did walk in meadows green
  I heard the summer noon resound
With call of myriad things unseen
  That leapt and crept upon the ground.

High overhead the windless air
  Throbbed with the homesick coursing cry
Of swallows that did everywhere
  Wake echo in the sky.

Beside me, too, clear waters coursed
  Which willow branches, lapsing low,
Breaking their crystal gliding forced
  To sing as they did flow.

I listened; and my heart was dumb
  With praise no language could express;
Longing in vain for him to come
  Who had breathed such blessedness.

On this fair world, wherein we pass
   So chequered and so brief a stay;
And yearned in spirit to learn, alas,
   What kept him still away.

THE FLIGHT

How do the days press on, and lay
Their fallen locks at evening down,
Whileas the stars in darkness play
And moonbeams weave a crown—

A crown of flower-like light in heaven,
Where in the hollow arch of space
Morn's mistress dreams, and the Pleiads seven
Stand watch about her place.

Stand watch—O days no number keep
Of hours when this dark clay is blind.
When the world's clocks are dumb in sleep
'Tis then I seek my kind.

THE TWO HOUSES

In the strange city of Life
  Two houses I know well:
One wherein Silence a garden hath,
  And one where Dark doth dwell.

Roof unto roof they stand,
  Shadowing the dizzied street,
Where Vanity flaunts her gilded booths
  In the noontide glare and heat.

Green-graped upon their walls
  An ancient hoary vine
Hath clustered their carven, lichenous stones
  With tendril serpentine.

And ever and anon,
  Dazed in that clamorous throng,
I thirst for the soundless fount that stills
  Those orchards mute of song.

Knock, knock, nor knock in vain:
  Heart all thy secrets tell
Where Silence a fast-sealed garden hath,
  Where Dark doth dwell.

FOR ALL THE GRIEF

FOR all the grief I have given with words
May now a few clear flowers blow,
In the dust, and the heat, and the silence of
    birds,
        Where the lonely go.

For the thing unsaid that heart asked of me
Be a dark, cool water calling—calling
To the footsore, benighted, solitary,
        When the shadows are falling.

O, be beauty for all my blindness,
A moon in the air where the weary wend,
And dews burdened with loving-kindness
        In the dark of the end.

THE SCRIBE

What lovely things
Thy hand hath made:
The smooth-plumed bird
In its emerald shade,
The seed of the grass,
The speck of stone
Which the wayfaring ant
Stirs—and hastes on!

Though I should sit
By some tarn in thy hills,
Using its ink
As the spirit wills
To write of Earth's wonders,
Its live, willed things,
Flit would the ages
On soundless wings
Ere unto Z

My pen drew nigh;
Leviathan told,
And the honey-fly:
And still would remain
My wit to try—
My worn reeds broken,
The dark tarn dry,
All words forgotten—
Thou, Lord, and I.

FARE WELL

When I lie where shades of darkness
Shall no more assail mine eyes,
Nor the rain make lamentation
　　When the wind sighs;
How will fare the world whose wonder
Was the very proof of me?
Memory fades, must the remembered
　　Perishing be?

Oh, when this my dust surrenders
Hand, foot, lip, to dust again,
May these loved and loving faces
　　Please other men!
May the rusting harvest hedgerow
Still the Traveller's Joy entwine,
And as happy children gather
　　Posies once mine.

Look thy last on all things lovely,
Every hour.   Let no night
Seal thy sense in deathly slumber
     Till to delight
Thou have paid thy utmost blessing;
Since that all things thou wouldst praise
Beauty took from those who loved them
     In other days.

BY WALTER DE LA MARE

PEACOCK PIE

Illustrated by W. Heath Robinson. $2.00 net

There is always a suggestion of magic about Mr. De la Mare's poems. From a simple beginning, the reader is suddenly lifted out of the tangible into something a little beyond his grasp. This magic lies not so much in what Mr. De la Mare says as the voice in which he says it and the gesture which accompanies it.

"*Peacock Pie* is the most authentic knapsack of fairy gold since the *Child's Garden of Verses*. One's first thought is that it is a collection of poems for children. But before you have gone very far you will find that the imaginary child you set out with has been magicked into a changeling. When, at last, you have finished, it will be with the sigh of one who has been thrilled through and through.

"One may well despair of conveying in a few rough paragraphs the gist of this quaint, fanciful, brooding charm. There is something fey about much of the book. In its love of children, its inspired simplicity, its sparkle of whim and Æsopian brevity, I know of nothing finer."
—C. D. M., in *The Boston Transcript.*

THE LISTENERS

$1.20 net

Of *The Listeners, The Providence Journal* said: "Rarely does one come across so lovely a wind-flower of verse. One feels one has in truth entered the enchanted country."

HENRY HOLT AND COMPANY
PUBLISHERS   NEW YORK